JIMMY EVANS

THE
SECRET
POWER
OF SEXUAL
PURITY

Family and Marriage
Today™
P.O. Box 8400
Amarillo, TX 79114

All examples in this book involving ministry situations are real. However, the details and surrounding circumstances may have been altered or combined to preserve the privacy and confidentiality of the individuals involved.

For simplicity, the masculine pronoun is used when speaking in general terms; it is intended to be interchangeable with the feminine.

All Scripture quotations are from the New King James Version (NKJV), copyright © 1979, 1980, 1982, Thomas Nelson, Inc., Publishers, unless otherwise noted.

ISBN 0-9647435-3-1
10 9 8 7 6 5 4 3 2 1
Printed in the United States of America.

CONTENTS

INTRODUCTION

As a pastor for eighteen years, I have ministered to hundreds of men individually and to thousands of men in groups. One of the universal struggles men are dealing with is unprecedented sexual temptation. We live in a world of sexual imagery and seduction; these influences are everywhere we turn. As men, we are visually aroused when it comes to sex. Capitalizing on this, advertisers, entertainers, and porn peddlers bombard us with sexual images they know will attract us.

Whether it's television, magazines, computers, movies, billboards, or just a pretty girl walking down the street, our minds are being deluged with images that have the potential of destroying our lives. I can't count the number of men I know whose lives have been deeply scarred, or whose marriages have ended in divorce because of sexual sin. In every case, the sin that ultimately damaged a life or destroyed a marriage and family began with the silent, private acceptance of sexual thoughts and images that were wrong.

One of the hallmark features of sexual sin is that of escalation. Anyone who believes sin truly satisfies is deceived. Sexual sin, whether mental, visual, or physical, begins a downward spiral of diminishing satisfaction and demand for greater stimulation. What previously satisfied is no longer enough. Once hooked, a man must live to satisfy the proverbial monkey on his back. Then, what was designed by God to be a beautiful, satisfying act of love between a husband and wife is reduced to a raw animal function. Devoid of anything sacred, sex becomes a self-centered pleasure fix, and women become objects to satisfy an insatiable sexual appetite. And so goes the dark tunnel that descends into the abyss of sexual bondage.

Even though men are the largest group dealing with sexual temptation and bondage, women are certainly not immune. Just as pornography is a multi-billion dollar industry oriented toward men, there are billions of dollars spent to attract women as well. Unlike men, women aren't as visual when it comes to sex. Even though women are certainly not blind to physical attractiveness, their sexual arousal is mainly connected to their emotions. Therefore, soap operas, romance novels, movies, television programs, and magazine articles court women's sexual interests on a daily basis. Even though these may be less graphic than male-oriented pornography, they are no less dangerous.

The sexual fantasies and lies being showered upon women today create deep deceptions and unrealistic expectations that can never be met in real life—just like pornography creates in men. The result for many women is the tendency to enter relationships with deceptive thinking that leads to greater frustration and disappointment, as well as the inclination for some married women to look for emotional and/or sexual satisfaction apart from their spouses. Just like men, women are being sexually tempted in an unprecedented manner. They are being courted by well-produced, highly attractive entertainment of every type to capture their sexual imagination and to lure their fallen nature.

When women accept the information being designed to appeal to them—regardless of how pleasant or entertaining—they are petting a hungry lion. I have witnessed unspeakable pain, as well as many divorces and incredible family devastation caused by the sinful sexual behavior of deceived women.

Regardless of the sexual differences between men and women, the answer to sexual temptation and bondage is the same. That answer is biblical meditation. I know that may surprise you and even seem a little simplistic when it comes to stopping the raging power of sexual impulses, but it is true. I know from experience—personally, and as a pastor.

While growing up, I lived in a normal middle-class neighborhood. I spent most of my time playing with the kids who lived on my block. We were typical for our age. Then one day, a neighbor friend down the street brought his father's *Playboy* magazine for us to look at. It was the first time I had seen a naked female.

I was perplexed and aroused. From that time on, he brought his father's magazines for us to examine on a regular basis. It was the beginning of a long season in my life of sexual temptation and deception.

As I got older, I was exposed to raunchier material than *Playboy.* In fact, *Playboy* seemed mild compared to many of the things I saw, especially in college. At one party I attended in college, an XXX-rated film was shown. Again, it was the first time I had seen anything like it. Not only was I aroused, but I was also fascinated by the women in it. They were sexually aggressive and totally uninhibited. This film fixed in my mind a deep deception about women and sex that had a very negative impact on my marriage in our early years.

In spite of my inner sexual battle, I received Christ as Lord of my life when I was nineteen years old. I have sought and served the Lord for the past twenty-seven years. I love Jesus and would never go back to the way I lived before. He has transformed me. One of the most powerful changes that has taken place in me is in the area of sex. Not only do I think much differently about sex today than I did when I was younger, but I am also free from the bondages and driving impulses of sex that were so powerful and prominent in my life back then.

It's important to understand that the transformation in me didn't happen automatically when I got saved. In fact, for years after receiving Christ, I still dealt with very strong sexual deceptions and temptations. Even though I was faithful to my wife and never fell into a bondage to pornography, it was attractive to me and very tempting. I wrestled constantly with my thought life and experienced nagging guilt and condemnation because of my inability to stop the thoughts I knew were wrong.

When I was in my mid-twenties, I was praying again for God to deliver me from the sexual desires and thoughts that were controlling me and keeping me from seeking and serving Him the way I desired. Soon after that, on a family vacation in Colorado, I noticed a small booklet lying on the coffee table in the house where we were staying. It was called *Biblical Meditation: A Transforming Discipline*, by Ronald A. Jensen.

As I picked it up and started reading, I was surprised by what I read. I don't know what I expected, but I certainly didn't think by looking at the cover that it was a booklet dealing with issues such as pornography, lust, and sexual temptation—but it was. The author was a seminary president who had wrestled with lust for most of his life. He explained how biblical meditation was the only thing that had ever set him free from sexual temptation and bondage. I was fascinated as I read what he had to say. I had tried everything to be set free sexually. I had tried casting demons out of myself, taking cold showers, removing television from our house, groveling repentance to God after every bout of sexual weakness—and nothing worked. What would I lose from trying biblical meditation?

Even though I had read the Bible on many occasions and studied it diligently as a young Christian, I had never meditated on Scripture

as a practice. As I began, my life was transformed, and the vicious cycle of sexual temptation and defeat ended. I was shocked at how
powerful biblical meditation was, and how
quickly it worked.

Over the years, I have walked in sexual victory, but I have never had a season in my life
when I wasn't sexually tempted on some level.
I say this so you won't think that biblical meditation removes the problem forever or guaran-
tees you'll never be tempted again. No. But
biblical meditation offers you a constant answer
to Satan's constant attack against you. When
you don't meditate, you are weak and more vulnerable to temptation and sin. When you meditate, you have the power to overcome and experience the victory promised by God for the one
who meditates in His Word. It isn't a one-time,
instant cure. It is a lifetime discipline that leads
to a lifetime of freedom and peace.

Whether you are married or single, man or
woman, young or old, I offer this information
on biblical meditation to you as something that
has changed my life and the lives of many oth-

ers I have counseled and taught over the years. It works.

Regardless of how seriously you have sinned, or how dark your past has been, you are invited to enter into the light of God's Word that can heal you, transform you from the inside out, and empower you to live in victory. Also, the power of biblical meditation reaches far beyond the issue of sexual sin. This discipline touches and transforms all areas of life—fear, depression, anger, confusion, addiction, and many other issues we all deal with.

The secret power for true freedom and victorious living is at your fingertips. Welcome to the transforming discipline of biblical meditation.

"How can a young man cleanse his way?

By taking heed according to Your word.

With my whole heart I have sought You;

Oh, let me not wander from

Your commandments!

Your word I have hidden in my heart,

That I might not sin against You!"

Psalm 119:9-11

"It is written, 'Man shall not live by

bread alone, but by every word that

proceeds from the mouth of God.' "

Jesus – Matthew 4:4

Chapter 1

ENTER THE BATTLEFIELD

THE
SECRET
POWER
OF SEXUAL
PURITY

When they crucified Jesus, they nailed Him to a cross and placed it on a hill called Golgotha. Golgotha means "the place of a skull." I've been to Jerusalem and seen Golgotha. It is eerie. As you view this hill from a distance, it looks just like a human skull. Therefore, on the day Jesus was crucified, He was hanging on a cross, positioned prominently on the top of a hill shaped like a skull. This was no accident. It was divinely orchestrated by God to reveal a central truth of the reason Christ died.

To understand sexual freedom or any other kind of freedom, we must realize that the battlefield of victory is the mind. This is why God chose the setting for the crucifixion as a place that had the name and appearance of a human skull. He could have chosen a hill that looked like an eye, heart, arm, or foot, but He didn't. Jesus died on the top of a skull-shaped hill to dramatically demonstrate the purpose of His death. Once His mission was accomplished, and He breathed His last, they pierced

Him in the side; blood and water spilled out and landed on the ground they called "a skull."

This powerful picture cannot be overlooked. You see, Jesus died to save us and set us free. Our minds are a central issue in the battle for our salvation and resulting freedom. The truth of the matter is, until our minds are set free, we're not free. Until the transforming power of the blood of Jesus and the water of His Word flow upon our minds, we are in bondage.

Francis Frangipane once said, "A bondage is a house of thoughts."

This is a truth we must understand if we are going to win the battle for freedom. Related to sexual bondage, many people think the issue is primarily biological or hormonal. Therefore, they try to fight their sexual impulses through physical discipline or willpower. Even the strongest person with the greatest amount of willpower can only last for a certain period of time until he or she is worn down by the force of sexual temptation. Thousands of years of human history prove that sexual sin can take the best people down. The story of David and Bathsheba demonstrates this point (2 Samuel, Chapter 11).

To solve a problem, you have to deal with the root issue before you can find a real solution. In other words, if you have a problem but are unaware of the true source of it, either you will try false answers that don't work, or you will believe that no answer exists. This is the predicament for most people related to sexual problems. They either try false answers that only have a temporary effect on their behavior, or they give themselves over to their sinful desires, believing that no solution exists because everything they tried failed.

In the area of sexual temptation and bondage, you will never be set free until you deal with the root issue, realizing the problem isn't primarily physical, hormonal, or the devil. The real problem is the way you think. Here is what Jesus said concerning freedom:

"Then Jesus said to those Jews who believed Him, 'If you abide in

My word, you are My disciples indeed.
And you shall know the truth,
and the truth shall make you free.' "

John 8:31-32

Jesus clearly stated in these verses that true freedom is the result of abiding in His Word. He promised that if we become committed disciples of His Word, we will "know" the truth, and the result will be freedom. The word "know" in the Greek language doesn't just mean "to understand." It means "to experience intimately." Therefore, Jesus promised that if we will commit our minds and hearts to His Word, the result will be a personal experience that sets us free.

Freedom is available for anyone in any bondage or battle of life. However, it must take place in our minds. Many people try and fail when it comes to changing a behavior or stopping a sin in their lives because they rely on their will instead of their minds. Sure, the will has to be involved; but it can't work independently from our minds or override the powerful force of our thoughts.

Again, as demonstrated on Golgotha, the central stage to obtain freedom is in the battlefield of our minds. The stage was set all the way back in Genesis, Chapter 3, when Satan first attacked mankind in the Garden of Eden. He didn't defeat them with bombs, guns or physical force. Satan's weapon of choice then and now is mental deception. As a cunning serpent, he seeks to silently introduce seductive thoughts into our minds that we will accept. A perfect example is pornography. Satan presents his destructive deception in a package that is enticing. However, even though you might not realize it, pornography isn't about nakedness, beautiful women, or sex. It's a multi-layered system of deceptive thinking that refutes God's Word and His will concerning the sacred nature of sex, the character of God, the role of men and women, the marriage covenant, love, and human fulfillment. Until we realize what pornography is really about and attack the central thought system behind it, we will never be free.

We also need to realize that the battle isn't between us and the devil. Even though our minds are the battlefield, the real fight is between God's Word and Satan. As long as we think the issue is about us, we will try to fight it ourselves. We must understand that we are helpless against Satan without God's Word. Ephesians 6:17 tells us that the Word is our "sword of the Spirit" in our fight against the forces of darkness. Even if we hate the enemy and are willing to fight, without God's Word, we are doomed to defeat and bondage.

Someone might be thinking, "Well, I know a lot of people who aren't religious and don't believe in the Bible, and they aren't in bondage to sex or things like that." Sure, not everyone in the world has the same bondages. However, you show me a person who doesn't live with a close, personal dependence upon God's Word, and I'll show you someone who is defeated and in bondage. The bondage might not be sex, but it's fear, depression, hate, or something else. No one is the exception—not even Jesus.

Matthew, Chapter 4, records the temptation of Christ after forty days of fasting in the wilderness. In His weakest moment, Satan appeared to defeat the Son of God. What did he attack Him with? Thoughts! Three times Satan attacked Jesus with half-truths and seductive offers. Every time, Jesus countered with a response beginning with, "It is written." Demonstrating the awesome power of God's Word over Satan's best attack, Jesus won and taught us how to do the same.

To help us understand the battle of our minds and how it is won, the Apostle Paul gives us rare spiritual insight in his second letter to the Corinthian church. He says, *"For though we walk in the flesh, we do not war according to the flesh. For the weapons of our warfare are not carnal but mighty in God for pulling down strongholds, casting down arguments and every high thing that exalts itself against the knowledge of God, <u>bringing every thought into captivity to the obedience of</u>*

Christ" (2 Corinthians 10:3-5, underline mine). These verses accurately describe the reality of the battlefield of our minds and the way to win the war for our freedom. Even though it's true, the greatest challenge of victory is the fact that the weapons and the war Paul describes can't be seen and must be entered into by faith.

Let's face it; it's hard for us to believe in the power of weapons that are invisible. It's also difficult for us to fight an enemy we can't see. However, that is exactly what we must do if we are going to live in victory. Paul tells us that we have weapons of warfare available for us that are "not carnal." Our weapons are not physical or natural; they are spiritual and invisible. He goes on to say that these weapons are "mighty in God for pulling down strongholds."

God has given us powerful spiritual weapons to overcome every stronghold Satan has brought into our lives to keep us in bondage. However, the power of these weapons will work only in an atmosphere of faith in which we are willing to obediently enter the battle of our minds.

Look again at Paul's language in 2 Corinthians 10. He tells us that we must bring "every thought captive to the obedience of Christ." This literally means that every thought in our minds must submit to the authority of Jesus Christ—the Word (John 1:1). Any thought we won't take captive will take us captive by building strongholds of "arguments" and "high things that exalt themselves against the knowledge of God." By faith, we must fight against any and every thought that won't bow its knee to Christ. These thoughts are our real enemy.

In the introduction to this book, I stated that the answer to sexual sin is biblical meditation. The Word of God is the only force powerful enough to destroy the strongholds of unrighteous thoughts that Satan introduces into our minds to hold us in bondage. It also acts as "sacred software" to reprogram us to function in the truth as God intended. The human brain is an amazing computer. However, we are all born with software problems, viruses, and glitches that only the Word can fix. The continuing process of biblical meditation as a discipline in our lives is crucial for freedom to be secured and maintained.

Hebrews 4:12 calls the Word of God a "two-edged sword." Each of the two edges serves a purpose; one of them destroys the enemy while the other acts as a surgeon's scalpel to heal us. The Word of God is able to reach into the deepest recesses of our minds, souls, and spirits—places we aren't even aware of on a conscious level, but which have a great influence on our lives. God's Word is a living, powerful force, but it has no effect until it gets inside of us.

The battle for freedom is waged in "the place of a skull." Until your mind is completely surrendered to Christ, and you are willing to seek and accept His Word as truth, you aren't ready for freedom and can't obtain it by any other means. However, if you're willing to bring your mind to Christ and cast down the arguments (thoughts that reject the truth of God's Word), surrender the high things (prideful thinking that believes it has a better answer than God's Word), and bring every thought captive, you are ready for freedom.

Jesus died on Golgotha—the place of a skull. Get it? Sure you do.

"I thought about my ways,
And turned my feet to Your testimonies."
Psalm 119:59

"Forever, O LORD,
Your word is settled in heaven.
Your faithfulness endures to all generations;
You established the earth, and it abides.
They continue this day according to
Your ordinances,
For all are Your servants.
Unless Your law had been my delight,
I would then have perished in my affliction.
I will never forget Your precepts,
For by them You have given me life.

I am Yours, save me;
For I have sought Your precepts.
The wicked wait for me to destroy me,
But I will consider Your testimonies."

Psalm 119:89-95

"Oh, how I love Your law!
It is my meditation all the day."

Psalm 119:97

Chapter 2

THE SECRET
OF SATAN'S SUCCESS

THE
SECRET
POWER
OF SEXUAL
PURITY

The battle for sexual purity is constant. Satan, the father of lies, is relentless in his efforts to deceive, seduce, and oppress our minds. If we are going to live victoriously, we must understand how to prevent him from successfully defeating us as he has countless souls before us. As we learned in the last chapter, the battlefield of sexual purity is our minds. Satan's weapons of attack are seductive words and thoughts that disagree with God's Word and will. According to the sixth chapter of Ephesians, God's Word, the "sword of the Spirit," is the only offensive weapon we have in our battle for freedom.

In this chapter, I want to unveil another dimension of the struggle for sexual purity and outline how to encounter it successfully. This dimension has to do with the way Satan attacks our minds and the secret of his success. Even though the devil has a great deal of experience tempting people, he really isn't very creative. With his record of success, he doesn't have to be. The same old tricks keep working for him.

But a closer look at Satan's temptations will give us insight as to how we can counter his attacks with a successful defense to keep ourselves sexually pure.

Satan's temptations always begin with a thought that is contrary to the standard of God's Word. Again, his methods have never changed. Satan's first words to man as recorded in Genesis, Chapter 3, were, "Has God surely said...?" Mocking the integrity of God and His Word, Satan began a deceptive barrage upon Eve that led to the fall of mankind. In the process of tempting Eve, he convinced her that God was a bully who was keeping her from realizing her potential. He also told Eve in no uncertain terms that the penalty of death God had posted for eating the forbidden fruit was false. She believed Satan and ate. The results were devastating. This is the continuing pattern of sin that has never changed throughout human history.

Satan is a liar, and he lies to you every day whether you realize it or not. He has two basic lies that never change. His first lie has to do with God's motives. He wants you to believe that God's Word is a legalistic standard from an uncaring, authoritarian God who is trying to keep you from enjoying life and fulfilling your potential.

If you accept that lie, you are ripe for the second one. He wants you to believe there will be no serious penalty if you decide to break God's laws. He will show you people on television and in the movies, as well as professional athletes and everyday people, who are living in sin and doing very well—at least it appears that way from a distance. He also keeps a few miserable-looking religious people handy to show you what will happen if you decide to obey God. Satan goes to great lengths to glamorize rebellion and to indict obedience to God because, you see, he really needs you to believe his second lie if he is going to be able to destroy you.

If we were honest, most of us would have to admit that we have a basic disagreement with the standards of God's Word related to sex. This is a pretty obvious point with all of the immorality in the world today. It's not a hard sell for the devil to get most of us to sin, because we have a basic beef with God's moral parameters. Some of you reading this may have never given it deep thought or been truly honest with yourselves; but really, what do you believe? Do you really believe what the Bible says about sex? Do you believe that sex outside of marriage is wrong? Do you believe God had your best interests in mind when He put parameters on sex, or do you believe He is prudish? Do you believe what Jesus said about a lustful look being the same in God's eyes as committing adultery? Do you believe that's fair? Do you believe "being in love" justifies sexual sin? Do you believe it's possible to live in sexual purity? Do you believe that sexual sin leads to serious consequences as God's Word promises? Be honest; what do you believe?

This point is so important because the Word of God is our primary weapon to fight the battle for sexual purity. However, it only works if we believe in it. Using military imagery, the Apostle Paul in Ephesians, Chapter 6, refers to our spiritual warfare against Satan. There he warns us that we must put on the whole armor of God daily to be able to stand against the schemes of the devil and his forces. In his description of the armor of God available to us, he tells us about several weapons that are important, but two that are critical. According to Paul, when we are fighting evil, one of our spiritual hands must wield the Word of God, the "sword of the Spirit," while the other holds "the shield of faith." Faith and God's Word must go together. One doesn't work without the other. You see, we will never defeat an enemy without a weapon or with one in which we have no faith.

Satan has six thousand years of experience at reading human doubts, indecision, and sympathy toward sin. Our behavior tells on us. Once he has mapped our weaknesses, he exploits them through enticing words and thoughts. When we allow him to do this without wielding our swords and shields, we have surrendered to him, whether we realize it or not. This was why Adam and Eve fell. Even though Eve put up a lame struggle when Satan accused God, she didn't fight for long. There were seeds of doubt in her heart that Satan was more than happy to water and fertilize. This is what he does with all of us. He knows our doubts and true inner beliefs, and he takes his opportunity through them. THIS IS THE SECRET OF HIS SUCCESS!

Satan preys on people who haven't resolved their doubts about God and/or sin. Even if we are half-heartedly holding our swords, he knows we're no threat without our shields of faith. He makes short work of even so-called "Bible believing" or "committed" Christians, unless they are armed with the sword of the Word and the shield of faith and are ready to use them. If we are going to live in victory, we must put on the whole armor of God daily as Paul advised—especially the Word of God combined with faith.

The issue of faith in God's Word is one that is decided by our hearts more than our minds. To have faith, it isn't necessary to understand everything the Bible says or even to like it. The important thing is to believe in the character and integrity of God, His Word simply being the extension of it. Hebrews 11:6 says this: *"But without faith it is impossible to please Him, for he who comes to God must believe that He is, and that He is a rewarder of those who diligently seek Him."*

Jesus said that unless we come to God like children, we can't enter the Kingdom of Heaven (Mark 10:15). Children are trusting. If you tell them there is a tooth fairy that will give them money for a pulled tooth, the next thing you know, they're yanking out teeth. They believe without cynicism or intellectualization. This is what God expects from us concerning Himself. Hebrews 11:6 tells us the two things God insists on if we are going to please Him through our faith. First, we have to believe "He is." This simply means we believe in the presence of God as being real and personal, though invisible.

The second thing we must believe is the fact that God is a rewarder of those who seek

Him. In other words, there is great reward for seeking and serving the Lord. Satan wants us to believe God is unfair and uncaring. Therefore, he accuses God to us constantly. He knows if we believe his lies, we will run away from God and into Satan's snare. However, faith focuses on what the Bible says regarding God's loving nature and the great rewards He offers to those who put their faith in Him. Faith is motivated by the goodness and generosity of God to us, His children. Like a child's faith, our faith requires that we take God at His Word by simply acting as though He is with us and He is a good Father.

God is good. He gave His Word to lead us into success and to protect us from damage. In the area of sex, we need to remember who created it—God, not the devil. Out of His love and goodness, He gave us a beautiful and exciting gift to enjoy. To make sure His wonderful gift to us would reach its fullest potential, He created the marriage relationship as the place for sex to be enjoyed safely for a lifetime. I've been married for twenty-seven years and can testify to the pleasure and ever-increasing satisfaction of sex in marriage. Marriage is without doubt the only relationship that creates the foundation of commitment and trust necessary for sex to reach its fullest potential.

Today, many people don't believe this perspective. They believe marriage is a moral straightjacket that prevents the full expression of sexual pleasure. In many circles, sexual sin is touted as a virtue of enlightenment that is passionately defended. Of course, the greatest defenders are usually the most zealous before their first sexually transmitted disease, personal devastation, or divorce. However, over time, the truth is hard to deny. Old sinners are bad advertisements for Satan. They prove the undeniable fact that sin is empty and kills everything it touches—the body, the mind, emotions, relationships, families, marriages, and dreams.

So the next time Satan comes whispering something sweet in your ear about sin, don't believe him. With simple faith in God, pull out your sword with faith and use it against him. It's the only thing that works. To live in sexual purity, you must learn to vigilantly close the gaps of doubt and indecision in your heart with your shield of faith as you counter Satan's lies with the truth of God's Word. This is especially important in the days we live in because the earth is covered with so much rebellion against God.

I have gone into detail about this subject so some of you will understand why you are so vulnerable to sexual sin. You know very well it is wrong, and you even grieve over it after you've failed. However, whether you realize it or not, you have an inner sympathy toward sexual sin. Even though all of us are tempted sexually, not everyone has the same thinking about sex. If you would closely examine the inner values of those who regularly struggle with sexual sin compared to the values of those who don't struggle as often, you would find something different. People who consistently struggle with sexual sin are still trying to decide what they believe. They haven't yet made up their minds whether it is good or bad. Of course, on the outside they will usually admit it's wrong. However, the devil knows the truth about their real beliefs. Regardless of what they say, their inward sympathy toward sexual sin and doubts about God's Word let the enemy know that he has the open ear of a sleeping soldier.

Proverbs 8:13 tells us that *"the fear of the Lord is to hate evil..."* It's not enough to look at sin and make a token comment about it being wrong. To war successfully against any enemy, you must hate him. You must understand his evil nature and his desire to destroy you. You must believe in your cause and carry your sword with a focused zeal to win at any cost. I have seen many people struggle with sexual sin for years without victory. The common characteristic of most of them is indecision toward God and sin. They have never decided to totally put their faith in God, and likewise, have never resolved that sin is their enemy. In reality, they simply won't completely commit to either camp—God's or

Satan's—because they have friends on both sides of the battle line and are therefore inwardly conflicted.

The Bible refers to these people as double-minded. They try to play both sides of the street. The result is what Jesus referred to as being lukewarm. Here is what Jesus said to the church at Laodicea in Revelation 3:15-16: *"I know your works, that you are neither cold nor hot. I could wish you were cold or hot. So then, because you are lukewarm, and neither cold nor hot, I will vomit you out of My mouth."*

Lukewarmness is the result of combining hot and cold. Spiritually, lukewarmness is the result of combining faith in God with sin. Rather than making a wholehearted commitment to God, we dabble in sin and daydream about forbidden delights as we foster secret doubts about the Bible. That is repulsive to God. Jesus compared it to taking a drink of a lukewarm beverage. When we take a drink, we want it to be hot or cold. Our first reflex when something lukewarm comes into our mouth is to spit it out. Likewise, God will not accept our indecision as faith, our compromise as commitment, or our sympathy with sin as a sign of love. Until we are ready to "get hot," we are still loyal to the devil's camp and are helpless against him.

Again, let me ask you the question: What do you believe? Do you believe in the goodness of God? Do you believe He loves you? Do you believe His Word is designed to give you wisdom and to protect you from evil? Or do you believe God is unfair? Do you believe that sin will add pleasure to your life without serious consequences? Do you believe God will bless a sin under some circumstances because you are lonely or your needs aren't getting met? Really, what do you believe?

The devil fears a faith-filled believer and feeds on the double-minded. He is terrified of the person who sees him for who he is and comes against him with the sword of the Spirit. He knows he stands no chance against the blood-bought child of God who has experienced the love and mercy of God and has wholeheartedly committed to living for Him.

What has sin or Satan ever done for you? I know many of you are reading this book because you are hurting and need help. I want you to know God loves you and will forgive you of any sin. He has the power to heal you and set you free. He is a good God, and He is with you right now. However, without faith, it is impossible to experience what He has to offer you. Faith means you are willing to act upon what God's Word says, regardless of whether you understand all of it or feel good about it. Faith means obeying God because you have a child-like belief that He is with you personally and will reward you for your obedience.

You can win this battle, but you must put faith in God and His Word. God loves you and has sent His Word to bless and protect you. Satan hates you and sends his seductive lies to deceive and destroy you. The war is being fought in the battlefield of your mind. It is between God's Word and the devil's lies. Whose side are you on?

When you are willing to totally commit to

God's side and stop sympathizing with the enemy, you will then be able to move forward to victory!

*"He sent His word and healed them,
And delivered them from their destructions."*

Psalm 107:20

*"And do not be conformed
to this world, but be
transformed by the renewing of your mind,
that you may prove what is that good and
acceptable and perfect will of God."*

Romans 12:2

*"The thief does not come except to steal,
and to kill, and to destroy. I have come that
they may have life, and that they may have
it more abundantly."*

Jesus—John 10:10

Chapter 3

THE PROMISE OF BIBLICAL MEDITATION

THE
SECRET
POWER
OF SEXUAL
PURITY

The book of Psalms begins with this powerful description of the person who has committed his or her mind to biblical meditation:

"Blessed is the man
Who walks not in the counsel of the ungodly,
Nor stands in the path of sinners,
Nor sits in the seat of the scornful;
But his delight is in the law of the Lord,
And in His law he meditates day and night.
He shall be like a tree
Planted by the rivers of water,
That brings forth its fruit in its season,
Whose leaf also shall not wither;
And whatever he does shall prosper."

Psalm 1:1-3

The power of biblical meditation is so great that God promises everything we do will prosper if we will practice it "day and night." This is a promise too great to ignore. Can you imagine everything in your life prospering and succeeding? Psalm 1:3 compares a person who meditates on Scripture day and night to a tree planted by a river. The tree doesn't have to worry whether or not the rains come because it has a stable source of water to keep it healthy and fruitful. The result is guaranteed success—just as God promises all of us if we will meditate on Scripture.

Many people beat their way through life trying to make it. Unlike a tree by a river, they look and feel more like a bush in the desert. Failure and frustration become so common that the thought of guaranteed success seems like an unrealistic dream. However, it's not a dream; it's a promise. That promise comes with one condition: that you refuse ungodly counsel and meditate upon God's Word day and night. If biblical meditation was the most difficult thing you ever did in your life, wouldn't it be worthwhile if it guaranteed you success in everything you did—work, money, relationships, sex, etc.?

I want to give you some really good news. Not only does biblical meditation guarantee success, but it is also delightful, and you can do it. When I first heard about it, I thought to myself, "I don't think I can do that." I also thought, "I don't know if I *want* to do that!" I just couldn't imagine sitting around thinking about the Bible all of the time. Sure, I loved God and believed in the Bible, but to think about it all day and night—wow! I didn't think I was up to it. That was twenty years ago. Now, after many years of biblical meditation, I can't believe how hard it was *not* doing it. I regret every day of my unbelief and procrastination. It caused me so much needless defeat and suffering.

Misunderstanding the idea of biblical meditation scares most people away. They think it is either impractical or too spiritually difficult for them. The truth is, any man, woman, or child can meditate upon Scripture day and night. In this chapter, I will erase the myths and misunderstandings concerning this powerful practice. I will also give you practical information to demonstrate how you can do it in the midst of your demanding lifestyle.

I want you to know that regardless of what you've experienced in your past, your future can be full of great blessing and success. If you can just meet the condition set forth in Psalm, Chapter 1, God promises His blessing of success in everything you do. You owe it to yourself to consider this issue carefully because of the powerful blessings being offered through the discipline of biblical meditation.

One great blessing is the power to live in sexual purity. Let me share with you a powerful truth concerning your mind and sexual temptation. Did you know that you cannot take a thought out of your mind? That's right—it's impossible. This is why sexual temptation is so wearying to try to fight. An example is this: You are minding your own business as you're flipping through the television channels, and then all of a sudden there she is—a perfect ten!!! From head to toe, she is gorgeous and sexy, and she's looking at you with that wanting stare. You pause for a few minutes and take it all in. Later, you turn off the television and go to bed, but she is still in your mind.

You lie in bed thinking about her. Then you realize what you're doing is wrong, and you begin feeling guilty. However, you just can't get the thought of her out of your mind. The more you try, the worse it gets. In fact, the more you try, the more other thoughts of other sexual images begin to surface, and the battle is raging. Finally, you give in to a mental gallery of erotic images that arouses you. Defeated and guilty, you go to sleep, only to wake up to another day of the same futile battle. You want to live for God and be faithful to your wife, but can you ever be strong enough to overcome these thoughts that have conquered you for so long?

If you can relate to this, I have some good news for you. You can have the power to overcome these undesirable thoughts and to exercise complete control over your mind. To do so, you must remember this: You cannot take thoughts out of your mind, but you can crowd them out with more powerful thoughts. This is where biblical meditation comes in.

Most people wrestle constantly with their thought lives. Many times we know the things we think about are wrong, but we don't know how to stop them. It's not just sex. It can be worry, fear, anger, or many other issues. We don't ask for them; they're just there, waiting for us. To make matters worse, the more we try to stop thinking about them, the more they occupy our thinking. Satan loves this vicious cycle because he wants to turn our minds inward until they wear out, we give up, and he controls us. Efforts to change become futile, so we just give in and become like everyone else. This is also why so many people turn to alcohol, drugs, and/or escape through some form of pleasure or distraction. It is the only way they know to cope with their internal miseries.

Before I came into the ministry, I worked in my family's business. On my way to work every day, I passed a billboard for a swimming pool company. It was a very large sign with a woman in a swimsuit filling most of it. Whoever painted her wasn't just a good artist, but was also intimately familiar with the female body and went to great pains to include every detail. As I passed the sign each day, I looked. In fact, I became so distracted by the sign that I would slow down before I got to it, hoping to hit a red light so I could look longer. Finally, the image on that billboard became fixed in my mind whether I was sitting in front of it or not.

One morning as I was trying to pray and have a quiet time with the Lord, the image of that sign flashed in my mind. Satan loves to do this to Christians when they are trying to worship in church, read the Bible, or pray, because he doesn't want us to get close to God. When this image came into my mind, I confessed it to the Lord and told Him I didn't want to think about it anymore, but didn't know how to stop it.

The Lord spoke to my heart right then and said something that began my journey to freedom from sexual temptation. He said to me, "Whenever this thought or any other temptation comes into your mind, begin to meditate on My Word." From that moment on, I began overcoming sexual temptation. I'm not saying I never sinned again; I'm saying that I started a pattern of winning more battles than I lost by knowing how to win every time through meditating on Scripture. In the next chapter, I'll explain the process of meditation so you will understand it clearly. But what I want you to understand now is the truth that biblical meditation replaces bad thoughts with God's thoughts and is the secret power to overcoming sexual temptation.

You can't get bad thoughts out of your mind with your own thoughts or some method of mind control or distraction. If you do, your success will be short-lived, and the thoughts will come back with a greater fury than before. The only power that can truly set you free from sexual temptation or any other mental battle you face is biblical meditation. This is why God promises success for the person who has committed to doing it day and night.

Make up your mind right now that the next time a bad thought comes into your mind—sexual or otherwise—you are going to replace it with a Scripture. Even more important, you will realize that the more you meditate on Scripture *before* you are tempted, the less opportunity Satan has to tempt you in the first place. You see, biblical meditation fills your mind with God's Word. Therefore, it is no longer unoccupied and open for the enemy's attacks. As the old saying goes, "An idle mind is the devil's playground." In reality, an idle mind is the devil's battleground where he stalks and defeats his victims.

Another important issue is understanding how to practically meditate on the Word of God "day and night" as Psalm 1:2 describes. If you misunderstand this point, you will get discouraged and give up before you start. However, once you understand what God's Word is saying, you will realize its brilliance and practicality.

To understand this issue, let's look at something God said through Moses to the children of Israel as they were preparing to enter the Promised Land. Deuteronomy 6:4-7 records these words: *"Hear, O Israel: The LORD our*

God, the LORD is one! You shall love the LORD your God with all your heart, with all your soul, and with all your strength. And these words which I command you today shall be in your heart. You shall teach them diligently to your children, and shall talk of them when you sit in your house, when you walk by the way, when you lie down, and when you rise up."

God's first commandment to Israel was for them to love Him and His Word with their whole hearts. This goes back to the point of the previous chapter. You must totally commit yourself to God before you can live victoriously. The second thing God commanded the men of Israel to do was to diligently teach their children the Word of God. God still holds men responsible to train their children in the Word and ways of God (Ephesians 6:4).

The interesting thing about God's commandment to train children in the Word is that God detailed for them the four times of the day and night in which it was to be done. In Deuteronomy 6:7, God directed the men of Israel to teach their children His Word and to talk about it when they 1) were sitting in their houses, 2) were on their way somewhere, 3) rose up in the morning, and 4) went to bed at night.

Let's go beyond God's commandment of teaching children. Think about the times when you are tempted and struggle with your thoughts the most. I'll tell you when it is. It is when your mind is in an unoccupied and reflective mode. You probably don't have as much problem with your thoughts when you are busy at work or directly occupied by a task. It's not to say you can't have problems during those times; it's just not as common because you are mentally preoccupied.

The times our minds are most open to satanic assault are when we are sitting around our houses (channel surfing, web surfing, etc.); on our way somewhere (in the car looking at billboards, noticing the person in the car next to us, daydreaming); and lying in bed as we wake up and go to sleep (worrying about our problems, fantasizing about our sinful desires). Let me guess; you just got nailed, right? We all did.

God knew thousands of years ago before there were televisions, computers, cars, billboards, or anything else that we were most vulnerable four times of the day. He also knew those same four times were the best opportunities for us to meditate on Scripture as we learn it ourselves and teach it to our children. Needless to say, most people today don't live as God directed in Deuteronomy. That is why Satan has so much success in his attacks upon our minds. For hours each day, most of us sit in our homes and cars and lie in our beds with our minds vacant and vulnerable.

Meditating on God's Word "day and night" means we are committed to occupying our minds with the Word of God during the four reflective times of our day mentioned in Deuteronomy 6:7. This doesn't mean we are legalistic and can't watch television, rent a movie, surf the web, or listen to music. It just means that God's Word comes before any of those things and that when we encounter a sinful thought through television, computers, movies, or anything else, we take it captive and replace it with a Scripture we have readily waiting in our minds.

Once you grasp the truths of this chapter and begin putting them into practice, you will realize how powerful they are. Life is more pleasant and peaceful when you learn to meditate upon Scripture. You realize that you can defeat the enemy any time he comes against you and can live your life free from mental turmoil and sexual sin. You also realize the power of the Word of God. As you meditate on it, the Word unfolds within you, and you begin to see its beauty and understand its mysteries. The Bible is no longer a difficult book you have a hard time getting into. It becomes your life source, and you begin longing for it.

Most of what I know about the Bible, I have learned while driving in my car, sitting in my house, or lying in my bed meditating on a Scripture. Not only has my mind been protected by biblical meditation, but it also has been enlightened and prepared for success. Truly, biblical meditation has changed my life, and God has fulfilled His promise to prosper me in all of my ways. He will do the same for you too.

A promise of complete success awaits the person who commits to meditating on God's Word day and night. This promise is open for any man, woman, or child to claim. Like a tree planted by a river, any person who desires to plant his or her mind in God's Word will never have to worry because the future is settled. Victory and success are guaranteed!

"This Book of the Law
shall not depart from your
mouth, but you shall meditate
in it day and night, that
you may observe to do according
to all that is written in it.
For then you will make
your way prosperous, and then you
will have good success."

Joshua 1:8

"My soul shall be satisfied
as with marrow and fatness,
And my mouth shall praise
You with joyful lips.
When I remember You on my bed,
I meditate on You in the night watches."
Psalm 63:5-6

"I rise before the dawning of the morning,
And cry for help;
I hope in Your word.
My eyes are awake
through the night watches,
That I may meditate on Your word."
Psalm 119:147-148

"I rejoice at Your word
As one who finds great treasure."
Psalm 119:162

Chapter 4

THE PROCESS OF
BIBLICAL MEDITATION

THE
SECRET
POWER
OF SEXUAL
PURITY

I hope by this point you are sold on the need for biblical meditation. As I said in the previous chapter, it is a delightful discipline that adds a new dimension to life. Biblical meditation is not a religious ball and chain; instead, it is a practice that actually makes life much easier and more enjoyable. It isn't a burden—it's a blessing. I'm saying all of this to help you see it for what it really is and to encourage you to do whatever is necessary to establish it as a discipline in your life.

In this chapter, I'm going to show you how to practice biblical meditation in an easy, simple manner that you can custom fit to your need and lifestyle. Let's begin by understanding the word "meditate" as it is used in the Bible.

Obviously, we're not talking about meditation as it's practiced in Eastern religions or the New Age movement, which involve focusing the mind on self, some unknown cosmic power, or your choice of gods. Biblical meditation is mentally rehearsing a portion of

Scripture that in turn causes you to consider God and the things of God.

The word "meditate" as used in the Bible means two basic things. First, it means "to consider or ponder." Second, it means "to speak or murmur to oneself." A good picture of meditation is an animal such as a cow or sheep that chews its cud and "ruminates." Rumination is the process of chewing, swallowing, and then regurgitating to chew again.

A sheep has multiple stomachs. The process of rumination causes the grass the sheep is eating to be refined over and over until it passes into the final stomach and is digested in a pure form. Likewise, biblical meditation means to take a Bible verse, text, chapter, or story and put it into your mind. Then, throughout the day, you keep bringing it back into your mind as you keep mentally "chewing on it."

As I have meditated over the years, the Lord has revealed great truths in His Word that I had never seen by simply reading the Bible. As you meditate, the Word of God unfolds within you.

Just like rumination in sheep, meditation keeps refining Scripture within your spirit until it is digested in its pure form. You begin to see things in the Bible you've never seen before as it gives you a new level of wisdom, insight, and encouragement. Also, as I stated in the previous chapter, meditation powerfully protects your mind against lust, worry, fear, and every other attack Satan brings against you.

The appendix of this book lists some specific suggestions of Scriptures to meditate on when you are facing certain challenges. You really need to make meditation something that applies personally to your life. Suppose you are facing something at work that you're anxious about. It is causing you to lose sleep at night, have headaches, and deal with emotions that are in turmoil. This is a common scenario many people face.

Just as a physician prescribes specific medicine for a specific illness, you need to find a verse, text, or story in the Bible to meditate upon that will minister to you right where you are living. In the case of worry and anxiety, Matthew 6:25-34 is a Scripture in which Jesus admonishes us to trust God and not to worry. This would be a great text to meditate on to calm your heart, relax your body, and give you faith to trust God.

If meditation becomes some dry, religious exercise that doesn't apply to where you are living, you aren't going to do it. However, if it helps you find solutions, control your thoughts and emotions, as well as build a deeper relationship with God, it becomes much more desirable. That is the key to making it a permanent discipline in your life.

Another thing I love about biblical meditation is that you can do it anywhere at anytime, and it produces immediate results. On a plane, in a meeting, at the car wash, in bed, or anywhere, you can simply reflect upon Scripture and enjoy the presence and power of God instantly. With today's fast-paced, demanding schedules, this is important. Also, it removes any excuse of not being able to do it. The busiest person in the world can find times throughout the day to meditate.

The Bible is so wonderful. It addresses every issue of life and gives us Scriptures for knowledge, wisdom, encouragement, warning, and comfort. There's simply no other book like it. It is so practical, and it equips us to face everyday issues head-on and victoriously. The greatest tragedy is for a Bible to be gathering dust on the coffee table while its owner is getting tossed around by life and beat up by the devil.

I know right now you are facing some challenges in your life that are causing you anxiety and stress. I also know that the devil is attacking you in some area. In other words, I know you could be helped by biblical meditation right now. For that reason, in addition to what I have already shared, I will use the remainder of this chapter helping you understand some practical steps you can take to make it work in your life.

First of all, you need to have a Bible you can read and understand. There are many good translations of the Bible that are written in today's English. Examples are the New King

James, New American Standard, and the New Living Bible translation (not the paraphrase). These are all great translations. If you have a Bible that you have difficulty reading, such as the King James Version, don't feel guilty. It's just not written in language most of us can get into. Go to your local Christian bookstore, and buy a new Bible if you need one.

Another great help in biblical meditation is a Bible concordance. A concordance is kind of like a road map of the Bible that helps you find the Scriptures you are looking for. For example, suppose you're dealing with fear. You look up the word "fear" in the concordance, and it will show you every place in the Bible where "fear" occurs. It is very helpful. If possible, buy a concordance that corresponds to the translation of the Bible you are using.

There are also concordances that give the definitions to the original Greek and Hebrew words. These are powerful tools to aid in understanding what a verse really means. Christian bookstores today have many good Bibles and study tools. You just need to shop around and find something you like. It's well worth the time and money you will spend.

Once you have an understandable translation of the Bible (and concordance, if you can), the next step is to wake up a little earlier than normal and begin your day with a "quiet time." Some of you may be doing this already. A quiet time is simply a private time you spend alone with the Lord. If you can't do it at home for some reason, you can have a quiet time in your car or at the office. The main thing is to find a private place where you can spend some time reading your Bible and praying.

I know people who prefer to have their quiet times at night. That's fine, but you need to remember that biblical meditation is something you do throughout the day. If you have a quiet time at night, you need to make sure that you are preparing yourself for the next day and that when you wake up, you renew yourself in the Scripture(s) you are meditating upon. Mornings are a critical time in meditation. Rarely will you meditate during your day if you don't prepare yourself properly in the morning and set your mind to do it.

As a dear saint, Campbell McAlpine, once said, "Having our main time with the Lord at the end of the day is like tuning the instruments after the symphony is over." Prayer and Bible reading at any time are important and beneficial. However, you must remember that one of the main reasons to spend time reading the Bible and praying is to prepare you to live successfully. Therefore, the morning is a strategically important time for you to prepare to face your day with God and His Word as your allies.

A quiet time can last ten minutes or two hours. The main point is that you spend time reading the Bible and talking to the Lord about the issues of your life. Concerning biblical meditation, your quiet time is when you read a verse, story, or text of Scripture for the purpose of "loading" it into your mind for meditation through the day. Again, read what you need. Find something that applies to your life. If you don't have a pressing need, then find a Scripture you want to memorize or a verse you

don't understand that you want the Holy Spirit
to reveal to you. Also, if you're being tempted
or oppressed, find a Scripture that deals specif-
ically with that issue.

I love to find stories in the Bible that fas-
cinate me and meditate upon them—stories
like Daniel in the lion's den, David and
Goliath, Joseph's rise to power, and so many
others. The Bible is full of the most fascinat-
ing stories and information. There is always
something to help you in your life, your family, and your walk with God.

Once you have located a Scripture or text
in your quiet time, read it through several
times. Then pray for the Holy Spirit to give
you the power to meditate on it and to bring
it back to your mind at the right times. Also,
ask the Holy Spirit to reveal the Scripture to
your heart and make it alive to you. After
you've put the Scripture(s) in your mind and
prayed, you are then prepared to meditate
throughout the day and evening.

Remember what meditation means—to
ponder and/or murmur. Throughout the day as

you face temptations or when you are in a reflective time—sitting at a stoplight, lying in bed, or taking a coffee break at work—you simply bring the Scripture(s) back to mind and ponder it. Just like a sheep does, you bring it up and down to ruminate upon. As you do, the Word of God as the sword of the Spirit protects your mind against the devil's attacks. If you have a bad thought such as lust or worry, you can immediately replace it with the Scripture you are meditating on. In addition, meditation ministers God's peace to your mind as His Word becomes alive within you.

Meditation also includes singing or speaking. This is a great way to meditate, as well as an aid in memorizing Scripture. Ephesians 5:18-19 says; *"And do not be drunk with wine, in which is dissipation; but be filled with the Spirit, speaking to one another in psalms and hymns and spiritual songs, singing and making melody in your heart to the Lord."*

The presence of God powerfully inhabits His Word. Paul exhorts believers in Ephesians 5:18-19 to continually invite the Holy Spirit's presence into their lives by speaking or "murmuring" to one another with psalms, hymns, and spiritual songs from their hearts to God. A psalm is Scripture put to music, such as the book of Psalms. A hymn is a song about God and any issue concerning God, His kingdom, or an aspect of doctrine. A spiritual song is a new song that you sing personally to God from your own experience and relationship with Him. It is a very intimate sharing of love to God for who He is and for all the things He has done for you.

As you speak and sing psalms, hymns, or spiritual songs, you are meditating. As you do this, the Holy Spirit inhabits your words and praises. The result is a continual flow of the power and peace of God in your life. Truly, speaking and singing to yourself as you focus on God and His Word takes meditation to a higher level. Incorporating this as a habit as you go through your day is a pleasant and practical way to enforce the discipline of biblical meditation.

Meditation is simply thinking, contemplating, speaking, or singing to remind oneself of a Scripture or of God in general. It begins in the morning in your quiet time as you load your mind with a verse or text. As you pray for the Holy Spirit's help, you then spend your day bringing the Scripture(s) to mind. The most important times to do this are when you are being tempted or during one of the four reflective times of the day mentioned in the previous chapter. Also, beyond the foundation and beginning point of Scripture, meditation can and should at times blossom into a personal worship service in which you speak and sing to the Lord. The main issue is that God and His Word are occupying the central focus of your mind.

Psalm 1:3 issues an awesome promise for the person who meditates on God's Word day and night. The promise is success in everything he does. This simply means that if you begin your day by putting Scripture into your mind and then regularly reflect on it and rehearse it to yourself, you will be equipped to face any challenge of life successfully. Over time, your mind will be transformed. The result is thinking and behavior that is faith-filled, Bible-based, and victorious. All of this is the outcome of simply spending a few minutes in the morning and then some time here and there throughout the day and night "ruminating" on the Word.

Begin today right where you are. What issues are you facing? Where is Satan attacking you? I can promise you there is a Scripture that can empower you to overcome and succeed. It is waiting for you in the Bible. As you read it and then meditate upon it, you will enter into a new dimension of Christian living. You will find that meditating upon Scripture makes life much richer and more peaceful. You will also find that you are empowered to overcome Satan on every front, including sexual temptation. Rather than feeling like a helpless pawn on a sea of fate, you will feel like a well-armed soldier on the winning side.

"I call to remembrance
my song in the night;
I meditate within my heart,
And my spirit makes diligent search."

Psalm 77:6

"I will meditate on Your precepts,
And contemplate Your ways.
I will delight myself in Your statutes;
I will not forget Your word.
Deal bountifully with Your servant,
That I may live and keep Your word.
Open my eyes, that I may see
Wondrous things from Your law."

Psalm 119:15-18

Chapter 5

THE FOUR PILLARS OF MORAL INTEGRITY

THE
SECRET
POWER
OF SEXUAL
PURITY

So far in this book, I've focused on the main issue that determines whether we are able to overcome sexual temptation and live in freedom—biblical meditation. Even though it is the primary cause of sexual purity, it certainly isn't the only factor that sustains sexual and moral integrity. Without a doubt, biblical meditation is the foundation; however, there are also other supports that are critical in building a solid life of lasting integrity.

Besides biblical meditation, there are four other issues that are important to support and protect moral purity in our lives. I call these the four pillars of moral integrity. Laid upon the foundation of a submitted and pure mind, these pillars create a solid spiritual structure within us and around us that protects us from moral compromise. Also, when we are careful to establish these pillars, they promote strong relationships and lasting success in every area of our lives.

Moral integrity is becoming an increasingly rare commodity these days. Too many people have simply surrendered to the spirit of the age. The flood of sexual immorality we see around us every day is just one indication of the over-all moral decay of our society. In addition to sexual impurity, we are also being bombarded with spiritual deception, profanity, gossip, dis-loyalty, selfishness, materialism, rebellion, vio-lence, arrogance, and many other things that assault the standards of God's Word.

Without a conscious decision to reject the current all-out attack on biblical values and everything sacred, we too will be swept away in the sin that is swirling around us. Even if we pride ourselves in the fact that we are not as sinful as others, we nevertheless compro-mise ourselves when we accept standards for our lives that are below those of the Bible. In so doing, we also forfeit untold blessings and place ourselves squarely in harm's way.

Regardless of how pleasant sin can be for the moment or how popular it is, sin kills. Romans 6:23 says, *"For the wages of sin is death..."* This truth is stated in the present tense: *"...the wages of sin IS death..."* Sin instantly produces death in everything it touches—the mind, the body, a marriage, a relationship with God, and everything else. Anything precious in your life that you allow sin to touch, it will kill. You are wasting your time building a family, business, reputation, ministry, or anything else if you're not going to protect it from sin.

The word "integrity" means to be "whole" or "morally complete"; in other words, every area of your life is up to the necessary standard. Even if ninety-five percent of your life is in great shape, the five percent that is compromised can destroy the other ninety-five percent. The devil doesn't need you to give him every area of your life before he can destroy it, just like a burglar doesn't need you to leave every window and door open to rob you. One entry point is sufficient.

Many otherwise good people have been destroyed through sexual sin, financial dishonesty, or unrestrained temper. If you are justifying a five-percent sin ratio in your life because of the ninety-five percent that is good, you are being set up for destruction. That is exactly the mindset the devil loves. However, the real definition of integrity is "moral completeness" and "wholeness." This is the only definition that ensures lasting integrity and spiritual victory because it closes every door to the devil.

Moral integrity is a personal decision to respect the character of God and the destructive power of sin by creating the necessary safeguards to prevent sin from entering your life as much as it is possible. In deciding to live a life of sexual purity and overall moral integrity, there are four elements or "pillars" that you must establish and maintain. They are:

1. **ACCOUNTABILITY** – Proverbs 18:1 says, *"A man who isolates himself seeks his own desire; He rages against all wise judgment."*

This Scripture hits the nail on the head concerning the motives of people who isolate themselves from accountability; they seek their own desires. In other words, they're doing their own thing, not God's thing. Also, they argue against counsel and input. They don't ask for advice and won't take it if you offer it to them. These are two classic characteristics of the person who is headed for a moral train wreck.

Everyone needs accountability and input. Not only do these factors provide protection from temptation and sin, but they also supply a wealth of wisdom and greater perspective. As a pastor of a church of over six thousand people and a host of a national television ministry, I rarely go anywhere without being recognized. People often ask if that bothers me. I tell them quickly that I am thankful for such a high level of accountability and protection.

I love being accountable. I think I am one of the most blessed people in the world to have so many eyes watching me—some I know about and many I don't. Not only does it protect me from sin, but it also gives me an opportunity to be a witness for Christ because I'm being watched.

Besides the eyes of church members or television viewers, I am also directly accountable to the elders of our church and the board of our television ministry. In all, there are over thirty people to whom I give account related to my ministry and personal life. Words could never describe how much these people mean to me. Their input and accountability have protected me and enriched me in ways I could never express. Without a doubt, I would not be where I am today without them. They are gifts from God.

I cherish accountability as a blessing and a virtue. I also reject independence as a sin and a set-up for destruction. As a pastor and marriage counselor, I see many lives in a candid way others never see. One of the truths I have repeatedly observed in ministry to people is that personal, moral, and marriage failures always hatch out of the cocoon of independence and non-accountability.

On the other hand, those I see who are successful in life are accountable. They go to church and build relationships. They open their lives to spiritual leaders, experts, and close friends for examination and correction. They seek counsel when they are struggling or are making important decisions. Far from the cocoon of independence, these butterflies are free because they have broken from the darkness to live in the light.

Satan is the prince of darkness, and God is the Father of lights (James 1:17). They both perform their works in their respective environments—Satan in darkness and God in the light. Here is what Jesus said in John 3:19-21 about light and darkness and what it reveals about our hearts:

"And this is the condemnation, that the light has come into the world, and men loved darkness rather than light, because their deeds were evil. For everyone practicing evil hates the light and does not come to the light, lest his deeds should be exposed. But he who does the truth comes to the light, that his deeds may be clearly seen, that they have been done in God."

When people plan on doing something good or godly, they don't mind others watching because they are proud of their actions. However, when people are going to do something sinful, they hide themselves from scrutiny. People who plan on living righteously don't mind accountability. In fact, they seek it. However, refusing accountability is planning to sin and reveals one's true character. Moral integrity demands accountability.

2. **<u>RIGHTEOUS FELLOWSHIP</u>** –

1 Corinthians 15:33 says, *"Do not be deceived: 'Evil company corrupts good habits.'"* This issue has deceived many people. That's why this Scripture begins with a warning not to be deceived before it explains the dangers of evil company. This verse offers an eternal and universal truth—evil company corrupts good habits. This truth pertains to children and adults, men and women, Christians and non-Christians. However, many people believe they are the exception.

The important point of 1 Corinthians 15:33 is that bad company overcomes good habits. This is where many people are deceived. For example, some Christian parents who have diligently trained their children will allow them to run with a group of unrighteous, but popular, friends. Their justification many times is the deceived belief that their children will evangelize the others. I have comforted many heartbroken parents on the other end of this lie.

Many adults make the same mistake. They think they can closely associate with people who are living a sinful lifestyle without being affected. I have seen hundreds of Christian men and women leave their spouses and fall into immorality, drug abuse, alcohol abuse, and other sins because of the influence of a close relationship with an ungodly co-worker or friend.

Of course, we as Christians should befriend and evangelize non-Christians. However, our base of fellowship must be with those who share our values and faith in Christ. Evangelism reaches out from that base of Christian relationships to draw non-Christians into it. Never should we make our regular, close group of friends those who don't share our values and/or faith in Christ. The word "company" in 1 Corinthians 15:33 refers to regular fellowship or frequent companionship. Therefore, bad people aren't the issue; bad company is.

This is the truth: you will not be different than your close friends for long. If you run around with godly people, they have an effect on you. You are inspired to do better and to live higher because of their influence. Also, because their values are based on Christian principles, a moral protection is built in. This isn't to say Christians are always perfect or even better than non-Christians. But you must carefully choose all of the close friends you have (even Christians) because they will greatly influence your life—good or bad.

The issue of bad company also relates to the entertainment we choose and the environment of our homes. I enjoy watching television, but I am careful to avoid immoral programs. I realize you can't completely avoid anything negative, but you can certainly avoid most of it.

Television programs, movies, and computers are three mediums that provide great entertainment and education. However, they all have the potential for much evil. If you allow unrighteous television programs, movies, or Internet web sites into your life, you are eventually going to be corrupted by them, regardless of how good or godly a person you are. If you don't believe this or feel as though you are the exception, you are deceived just as 1 Corinthians 15:33 warned.

There is a saying that goes like this:

Sow a thought; reap an action.
Sow an action; reap a habit.
Sow a habit; reap a character.
Sow that character; reap a destiny.

Even though this saying isn't in the Bible, I believe it is true because of this Scripture that reinforces its message: *"Do not be deceived, God is not mocked; for whatever a man sows, that he will also reap. For he who sows to his flesh will of the flesh reap corruption, but he who sows to the Spirit will of the Spirit reap everlasting life"* (Galatians 6:7-8).

Every thought that comes into your mind plants a seed. We have already discussed how to overcome negative thoughts through biblical meditation. However, even though biblical meditation is powerful, God won't allow it to be used as a weed killer for the crop of unrighteous seeds you willingly invite into your mind. In other words, if you are going to see explicit movies, watch immoral television programs, and view pornography on the Internet, and then try to use biblical meditation as a quick fix, you're in for some bad news. It won't work. The only way to kill that crop is through repentance, which requires turning away from and changing your mind about sin.

If you are going to live in moral integrity, you must scrutinize what you allow to come into your mind. I'm not legalistic, but I have learned what forms of entertainment war in my mind against godly living, and I will not allow them in. All entertainment seeds our minds with thoughts that germinate and grow over time.

Don't be deceived; bad company will corrupt you. In every area of your life, you need to wisely choose your friends and entertainment, including music. Also, if you're struggling with Internet pornography or something else, confess it to a pastor or godly friend and become accountable. Don't be ashamed and don't allow it to remain in the darkness. Do everything necessary to create an environment of "good company" around you.

3. **HONESTY** – Jesus told us in John 8:32 that the truth would make us free. The other side of that is the fact that dishonesty keeps us in bondage. One of the worst parts of my job as a pastor is dealing with people who are caught in sin and are trying to justify it.

I know many "believers" who have committed adultery and, rather than repenting when they were caught, have calmly explained that God told them to do it. I have never met a hardened sinner who didn't have a justification for his or her behavior. In some cases, the blame is placed on someone else, such as a wife, husband, parent, boss, or the government. In other cases, people compare themselves to someone else and justify the sin because it's not nearly as bad as "so and so's." In other cases, they distort a Scripture or manufacture a voice from heaven to enable them to dress their sin in white and call it holy. In every case, though, they are living a lie.

John, Chapter 18, records the examination of Jesus by Pontius Pilate before His crucifixion. As Pilate questioned Him, Jesus said little. One thing He did say, though, concerned the issue of truth. Jesus said to Pilate in John 18:37, *"Everyone who is of the truth hears my voice."* Pilate sarcastically retorted, *"What is truth?"* (John 18:38).

Jesus' words are still true today. Everyone who is truly of God is willing to hear the truth from Jesus. Also, Jesus is the truth. This is what He told us in John 14:6: *"I am the way, the truth, and the life."* When

Pilate said, *"What is truth?"* he wasn't asking a question; he was expressing his belief that there was no absolute standard for truth. This is still the belief of many people, and it is how they rationalize sin and justify unrighteous behavior.

If you are going to live in moral integrity, you've got to decide what it means to you. For me, moral integrity means living according to the model of Jesus Christ and the standard of His Word. In a world of shifting-sand values that are constantly changing to fit the new definition of political correctness or popular opinion, the only stable and reliable standard is God's Word. According to Jesus, it is the only standard of eternal truth and the one by which we will be eternally judged. To believe anything else is to believe a lie, which ensures bondage, because only the truth can set you free.

Don't lie to yourself, and don't let anyone else, including the devil, tell you lies to justify sin in your life. Come into the light and accept the truth. That is the atmosphere in which God works and the devil is powerless. It is also the environment that ensures sexual purity and moral integrity.

4. **HUMILITY** – My friend's wife called me one morning, crying hysterically. In the background, I could hear her children crying and screaming, "Daddy, don't leave us." Through her sobs, she explained to me that her husband, my friend, was leaving her because of sex. I immediately asked her, "Is there another woman?" She replied, "No, he just wants more sex than I can give him, and he is leaving me to get it. Will you please talk to him?"

The next thing I heard was the phone drop and her voice begging her husband to talk to me. I had been friends with him for many years, and he had been instrumental in my spiritual development when I first came to Christ. It was difficult for me to comprehend what was happening in this moment, but it hadn't come completely without warning.

A couple of years before this phone call, my friend began withdrawing from me and other Christian relationships in his life. He also began working for a very unrighteous man with whom he traveled regularly for days at a time, away from his wife and children. I shared my concerns with him more than once about his increasing separation from his family and friends and especially about his close working relationship with his boss.

According to my friend, he was "temporarily" withdrawing from the relationships with me and other Christian friends because he was "in a busy season." Also, when I asked him about the close working relationship with his boss, he said he was "ministering" to him when they were on the road. The truth was, my friend was being "ministered" to by his boss. He began drinking, partying, and regularly watching adult movies in his motel rooms when they traveled. This began the fall that ultimately claimed his marriage, Christian witness, and ministry.

Back to the phone call: After a few minutes' wait, my friend picked up the phone. Without a shred of remorse in his voice, he excitedly told me that he was moving in with a friend to explore his expanded sexual interests. I couldn't believe my ears. With the sound of his children crying and screaming in the background, he calmly told me that his wife was perfect in every way, but she just didn't give him enough sex.

He went on to tell me that in the previous year, he had been sexually experimenting outside of his marriage and was convinced that he must divorce his wife to continue his pursuits. Above my arguments and the pleading of his wife and kids, he left that morning and never came back. This was the man who was my spiritual mentor just a few years earlier.

Proverbs 16:18 says, *"Pride goes before destruction, And a haughty spirit before a fall."* My friend was proud. He believed he could separate himself from righteous fellowship and Christian accountability and survive the influence of his unrighteous boss on the road. He was proud and foolish. The result was destruction.

I know I could fall morally. There isn't a

shadow of doubt in my mind that I am capable of any sin, apart from the grace of God. Because of that, I will not allow myself the arrogant assumption that I can break the rules and survive. If I break the rules, I'm history, and I know it.

Pride thinks it is capable of success apart from humble obedience to God and adherence to the standards of the Word. Just as my friend refused to listen when I cautioned him about his decision to separate from accountability and "minister" to his boss, pride won't listen. It won't admit its weaknesses. It won't seek counsel. It won't recognize the danger signs on the road to ruin. It won't do any of these things because it is intoxicated under the influence of arrogance.

You could fall. You need to admit it to yourself. Because of that, you need God and godly people around you. You need to walk carefully and realize that your enemy is prowling around, seeking an arrogant, careless soul to devour. If you're humble, you will escape him and live securely from his schemes. However, if you think you can tame him, you're his next meal.

Concerning this very point, James 4:6-7 says, *"But He gives more grace. Therefore He says: 'God resists the proud, but gives grace to the humble.' Therefore submit to God. Resist the devil and he will flee from you."* Humility submits itself to God and recognizes its need for God. Therefore, God promises honor and authority over the devil to the one who is humble.

However, God "resists" the proud. This literally means that He sets Himself as an enemy against them. You see, when you're walking in pride, the devil is the least of your worries; you've got God against you. For that reason, you will not succeed or prosper for long. God will make sure of it.

It is possible to live in sexual purity and moral integrity. It is simply a matter of making the right choices and then living to honor Christ. As you seek to do this, the Holy Spirit is with you to give you the power you need to live for God and to make any changes you need to make. Submit and surrender to Him daily. He will lead you to a wonderful and prosperous life of sexual purity and moral integrity. I pray God's blessings upon you and hope this book has been a source of encouragement and help.

Appendix

THE
SECRET
POWER
OF SEXUAL
PURITY

Here is a list of some suggested Scriptures you can meditate on in dealing with specific issues you may face. This is certainly not an exhaustive list. There are hundreds more verses besides these that will equip you for victory in every area of life. This list of Scriptures will give you a starting point in some of the common areas most of us face. I hope they are helpful to you.

<u>AREA OF NEED</u>:
<u>SUGGESTED SCRIPTURES</u>:

LUST/IMMORALITY
Psalm 101; 1 Corinthians 6:13-20
Proverbs 5:15-21; Proverbs 6:20-7:27

WORRY/ANXIETY
Philippians 4:6-7; Matthew 6:24-34
Matthew 11:28-30; Isaiah 40:31

FEAR
2 Timothy 1:7; Psalm 91; Isaiah 26:3

ANGER/UNFORGIVENESS
Ephesians 4:26-27; Matthew 18:21-35
Proverbs 14:17; Proverbs 15:1
1 Corinthians 13; Galatians 5:22-23

DISCOURAGEMENT
Galatians 6:9; Hebrews 12
Romans 5:3-5; Joshua 1:8-9

CONDEMNATION
Romans 8:1-4; 1 John 1:9
Revelation 12:10-11; Psalm 103:8-14
Ephesians 2:4-8; 2 Corinthians 12:9

INSECURITY
Philippians 4:13; Psalm 46:1-3

MARRIAGE PROBLEMS
Ephesians 5:21-33; 1 Peter 3:1-12

PRIDE
James 4:6-10; Mark 9:35
Matthew 23:11-12

FINANCIAL ISSUES
1 Timothy 6:6-12; Luke 12:13-21
Matthew 6:19-24; Proverbs 10:22
Malachi 3:8-12; Psalm 37